W9-BMO-074

Presented to

_____

by

_____

Date

When You Graduate

Charles L. Allen
and
Mouzon Biggs, Jr.

Inspirational Press ◆ New York

Contents

A Time to Commence 7
Shut the Gate 9
Eliminate Some Words 9
The Six Steps to Accomplish Your Dreams 10
My Excuse for Being Born 14
When You Feel Defeated 15
When the *New* Wears Thin 16
What Do You Most Desire? 27
Hope 28
Believe You Can 29
People—For Better or Worse 31
The Rhythm of All Life 38
Things Work Together for Good 39
Don't Be Afraid of the Gamble in Life 41
The Timid Souls 47
Blemishes Can Be Blessings 48
Get the Picture 50
Being a Person Who Makes a Difference 50
In God's Hand 59
The One Way 60

A Time to Commence

We think of graduation as the end of an era in our lives—and it is.

Graduation is also commencement. It is the time of beginning again.

In these pages, we have set down some principles which have been tried and proven in the experience of life. More important, we hope that this book will be an inspiration to seek new paths and gain new experiences. There is an old adage, "Beaten paths are for beaten people."

It has been well said, "A person who refuses the challenge of life has died without living."

CHARLES L. ALLEN
MOUZON BIGGS, JR.

Shut the Gate

One of the things that causes much unhappiness is the memory of past failures and defeats. The great Lord George of England on one occasion was walking through a pasture gate with a friend. He noticed that the friend did not shut the gate, so he went back and closed the gate, and then he said to his friend, "Never walk through a gate that you do not turn around and shut it." One of the essentials of a successful life is to be able to walk away from an experience, shut the gate behind you, and go on to something else.

Eliminate Some Words

One of the things we need to do is to eliminate some words from our vocabularies. The word we should start working to eliminate first is *impossible*. Jesus said, "All things are possible to him that believeth" (Mark 9:23). Jesus never used the word *impossible* one time. It was a word completely out of his vocabulary. Over and over, people have been defeated simply because they said, "It cannot be done."

I have told many people how to eliminate the word *impossible* from their vocabularies. It is a very simple method, and it usually takes just one week. Start tomorrow morning and keep a careful record of the times you say or think something cannot be done or cannot happen. Just before you go to bed, write down the number of times that thought came into your mind. Then concentrate on reducing the number of times the following day. By the end of the week, you will find that this negative approach just does not come to your mind at all. Then you begin thinking in terms of the possible. Someone coined the phrase, "the magic of belief." It is a marvelous experience to find out that belief truly is magic.

The Six Steps to Accomplish Your Dreams

Many years ago, a friend of mine said to me, "The word *impossible* is the most profane word in the English language." I would hardly put it that strongly, but the longer I live, the surer I am that one can accomplish one's dreams. Let's consider the six steps that can eliminate the word *impossible*.

1. *First,* decide what you really want. Many people go through life never getting anywhere because they never decide where they want to go. They never hit anything because they never shoot at anything. God gave us a marvelous mechanism called imagination. Just as a motion-picture camera can flash a picture onto a screen, so also can we put on the screen in our minds a picture of whatever we want to put there. Keep flashing the picture on the screen of your mind until it becomes clear and sharp.

2. *Second,* write down on paper your dominant desire. When you first write it out it may take a page, or even two or three pages, but then set to work to condense the idea. You must keep working until you can state your dream clearly in not more than fifty words. I have tried this many times, and I have been amazed at how much one can put into fifty words.

3. *Third,* after you have stated your idea in not more than fifty words, memorize it, and several times each day stand before a mirror and repeat it aloud. The first time I tried that I felt like a fool. But keep on doing it, and it is amazing how the idea will take possession of you. Study the lives of people who have accomplished great things and you will find some-where along the way that they became possessed by an idea.

This idea is in line with some of the wisest men of the ages. Emerson once said, "A man is what he thinks about all day long." Marcus Aurelius, the wisest of the ancient Romans, said, "Our life is what our thoughts make it." The Bible says, "For as he thinketh in his heart, so is he" (Prov. 23:7).

When you firmly set your mind on an idea, obstacles begin to get out of the way as that idea begins to become a reality.

4. *Fourth,* test your idea. Is it good for you? Is it fair to all other people concerned? Are you ready for it now? Do you honestly feel it is according to the will of God? Underneath all this thinking is the insistence that you must rid your life of selfishness. When you think only of yourself and live for yourself, you have destroyed the very reason for living. No person really begins to live until he or she begins to live for God and for others. This thinking is in line with the One who said, "He that loseth his life for my sake shall find it" (Matt. 10:39).

5. *Fifth,* after clarifying your thinking and thoroughly testing your motives and purposes, you are ready for the main thing—*begin to pray.* One of my favorite passages of Scripture is Mark 11:22-26.

And Jesus answering saith unto them, Have faith in God. For verily I say unto you, That whosoever shall say unto this mountain, Be thou removed, and be thou cast into the sea; and shall not doubt in his heart, but shall believe that those things which he saith shall come to pass; he shall have whatsoever he saith. Therefore I say unto you, What things soever ye desire, when ye pray, believe that ye receive them, and ye shall have them. And when you stand praying, forgive, if ye have ought against any: that your Father also which is in heaven may forgive you your trespasses. But if ye do not forgive, neither will your Father which is in heaven forgive your trespasses.

It is amazing what the reading of that passage will do for a person who is about to pray. I have watched pitchers warm up before a baseball game, and it is far more important to "warm up" before you begin to pray. That passage will warm you up and condition your mind in a marvelous manner.

It begins by telling you to have faith in God. Many things may be impossible in our own strength—but not with God. It talks about this business of moving mountains. Too often, we concentrate on our problems instead of on our powers. The passage ends with the injunction that if we expect God to hear us, we must have forgiveness in our hearts toward all people. Many times the power of God is blocked from life because God's spirit just will not share a heart that holds hates and grudges.

6. *Sixth* and last, you must do all you can toward accomplishing your desire. One day a friend phoned me to ask if I knew where he could get a typewriter. He had found a woman who needed help. He could have given her what she needed, and in many cases he did just give to one in need. But he discovered that this woman could type. So he set out to make it possible for her to earn what she needed. Many times God has done just that for us. Instead of giving us the answers to our prayers, He has given us the opportunities and abilities to answer our own prayers.

I have used these six principles in my own life, and I have observed the lives of others who have used them. I can say with assurance, that they really work for those who use them.

My Excuse for Being Born

The trouble with a lot of people was expressed by a little girl who lost her birth certificate. She cried to her teacher, "I've lost my excuse for being born." No person ever really finds his or her best in life until that person decides upon some reason why he or she was born.

A lot of people just drift along through life with nothing to live for and nothing important to do. George Bernard Shaw suggested that an appropriate epitaph for the tombstones of a lot of people would be: DIED AT 30, BURIED AT 60.

I knew a minister who was failing in his profession. He did not like being a minister. What he really wanted to do was open a garage and be a mechanic. He said, "The hum of a perfectly tuned motor sounds better to my ears than a church hymn." He would go to his study, but instead of studying, he would sit by the window and listen to the cars go by. When a motor was not running right, he would begin mentally checking what was wrong with it.

He felt that he was failing in life and burying his talents by doing what he thought he ought to do rather than what he really wanted to do. Then one day he decided that all work is sacred. He realized that one can tune a motor to the glory of God just as another can preach a sermon for God's glory. So he gave up the ministry and opened that garage. He found happiness in life and a purpose for living.

Usually, what you really want to do and what you ought to do are the same thing. God gave us certain talents, and a person likes to do what he or she can do well; and the thing you can do is usually the thing God planned for you to do. It really doesn't matter what your particular job is, just so long as it is the thing *you* are pleased with. If *you* are pleased with it, it is almost a cinch that God will be pleased with it as well.

◆

When You Feel Defeated

There is a man who once lived in America who inspires all of us, yet this man knew the meaning of defeat. His mother died when he was a child. As a young man, he ran for the legislature of his state, but he was defeated.

He entered business, but a worthless partner put him into bankruptcy. He fell passionately in love with a girl, but she died.

He served one term in Congress, but was defeated for reelection. He tried for an appointment to the United States Land Office, but failed to get it. He tried to be a lyceum lecturer, but he failed in that also.

He ran for the United States Senate, but was

defeated. He ran for vice-president of the United States, but was defeated.

His name was Abraham Lincoln.

When the *New* Wears Thin

A superintendent of a local Houston high school once invited me to address his graduating senior class. After attending a number of graduation ceremonies over a period of years, one begins to notice certain things that appear over and over again. I listen very carefully to the prayers and addresses at commencement exercises. The one word that I hear repeated more often than any other word is *new*. People talk about *new* opportunities, a *new* day, *new* horizons, a *new* threshold.

I've often wondered: Do people really want something new—*do* people want something new?

When I was in seminary, one of my professors told the following story. He was a delegate to a Methodist conference in Geneva. He decided to take his two teenaged sons with him on this important trip. After spending several days in Geneva, he and his sons moved south to Rome. He was looking forward to showing his sons the sights of Rome, particularly the beautiful art objects, paintings, and buildings. Finally, they came to the great church of St. Peter's.

While standing there, the man explaining different parts of the building to his sons, one of the boys pointed to the huge statue of St. Peter and said, "Hey, Dad, what happened to the big toe on his right foot?"

He didn't really remember any reference in the Bible to Simon Peter's having lost a big toe. He turned to a guide standing nearby and said, "What happened to the big toe on Simon Peter's right foot?"

The guide replied, "Well, sir, thousands of people come by this spot every year. I would guess that more than half stoop to kiss the foot of the statue, and over many, many years the saliva from human mouths has worn away the stone."

Why would people do that? Why? Because, I believe, people would do almost anything if they could imagine for a moment that life might be as new to them as they believe it was to that fisherman two thousand years ago.

In our own hemisphere, we have a beautiful story surrounding the church just northeast of Mexico City. It is called the Shrine of Guadalupe. The Shrine of Guadalupe has a very special mass each year on Christmas Eve. People come from many miles away to attend. Their particular custom is that on Christmas Eve everyone brings gifts of beautiful flowers as an offering to the Christ Child. One year, many years ago, a young Mexican boy wanted to go to that service, but he had no beautiful flowers. His family had no gardens and no money to buy flowers. The young boy had an idea. "Perhaps I could pull some of these weeds beside the path. When the people kneel at the altar to present the gifts of their flowers, it is very dark. Only the candles burn there. I could probably put these weeds alongside the beautiful flowers. No one would really know, and I could be there with all the other people." That's what he decided to do. At the appropriate moment, he knelt at the altar with hundreds of others who came with their flowers. As he pushed those weeds up onto the altar with a childlike faith, those who knelt nearby said that they began to glow in the candlelight with a strange, orange-red color. Mexico City had its first Christmas poinsettia.

Now, you and I say, "I don't want to hear that kind of story. I really don't want to hear that kind of story. This is a new day, a scientific day." We don't want to talk about weeds becoming poinsettias on the altar of a church. The real question is this: Why do people come, year after year, to deposit their flowers there? Because people will do almost anything for something new—a new kind of experience!

There is a little town not far from Houston called Port Neches, Texas. Little more than a year ago, a lady started out into her backyard late one afternoon. As she walked around in the backyard, she noticed something strange about the screen door on the back of her house. It had a shadow on it. She called her husband and said, "There is a shadow there unlike any shadow I've ever seen before."

Her husband said, "What do you think it is?"

She said, "It's the shadow of Jesus—the image of Christ." Now, you could ask right away, how did she know what Christ looked like? Well, she probably meant, "The shadow looks like some of the drawings I've seen of Jesus Christ."

Her husband agreed that the shadow did have a strange shape. However, he told his wife that once the sun had gone down, the shadow would disappear. The sun did go below the horizon, but the shadow was still there. This lady and her husband told their neighbors about the shadow, and they in turn told others. In three weeks, more than thirty thousand people walked through the backyard of that little home in a very small town in southeast Texas. Why? Because, I believe, people will do almost anything if they think something *new* is taking place. Once again you might say, "But you're talking about the church. People do weird things in the church. People do strange things in their religion." But none of us is really exempt from this search for something new.

Not long ago, I needed a new suit. One day I started down the street from our church. I walked into a men's clothing store. A gentleman said, "Can I help you, sir?"

I said, "Yes, I'd like to see a suit—size forty-two long." Before I could say anything else, he jerked several suits down from a rack and spread all of them out on a big, long table. Every coat was double-breasted. I quickly said, "Wait a second! I don't want a double-breasted coat."

"Why not?" he said.

"Well, I don't know," I answered. "I just don't particularly like double-breasted coats. Show me something else."

The guy leaned across the table and said, "Do you

know what? I don't like double-breasted coats either."

I said, "If I don't like double-breasted coats, and you don't particularly like double-breasted coats, why are you selling so many of them?"

The salesman replied, "Oh, that's easy. We have a whole new generation that has never worn a double-breasted coat, and they are looking for something new."

Each year in February I am invited to give the invocation at one of the performances of the rodeo at the Astrodome in Houston. I've prayed for some rather strange acts. Over the past years, I've prayed for the Beverly Hillbillies, Little Joe Cartwright, Johnny Cash, and Elvis Presley. I remember another time when I was fairly close to Elvis Presley. Oh, he wasn't my personal friend. It was when I was in high school in Carthage, Texas. It was a big day in Carthage, when a new feed mill was opened on the outskirts of town. The local persons who owned the feed mill wanted to be sure they would have a big crowd of people there to see them push the buttons and start the grinders. To ensure having a large crowd, the owners of the feed mill went to the Louisiana Hayride in Shreveport and hired a young singer by the name of Elvis Presley. The next week, the whole town was talking about Elvis Presley and his sideburns. Then what happened? Almost every boy in our high school started trying to let his sideburns grow. What did we do? We let them grow for two or three years, then we shaved them off. The only problem is that sideburns are not new. Neither are double-breasted coats. We've had them both before.

But don't let the ladies laugh at us. The ladies have short skirts, medium skirts, long skirts, high-heeled shoes, low-heeled shoes, medium-heeled shoes, pointed-toe shoes, squared-toe shoes—because *all* of us are looking for something new. We do want something new, don't we?

My second idea along this line is that we not only *want* something new, but we *need* something new. We really need a new day, new cities, new ideas, new dreams—or at least the realization of old dreams never fulfilled. Houston, Texas, is a wonderful place to live. And yet, we average almost one murder every day, hundreds of robberies every day; people being hurt, embarrassed, ignored, defeated, every day. We need something new!

Graduation looks like a new day. But I'm afraid you might be disappointed when you don't really feel very different the morning after graduation. Tuesdays start looking like Thursdays. Wednesdays look like Fridays. July and August look very much like they did last year. But we do need something new, don't we? We have said things to our parents that we really wish we had not said. We have done things to our classmates that we wish we had not done. We have wasted hours that we wish we could reclaim. We do want something new, and we do need something new. Is anything really new?

I have a psychiatrist friend in Houston. Several months ago he asked, "Do you know what month of the year I have more new patients than any other month?" I could not guess. Finally, he said, "It's

September." September—why would a psychiatrist have more new patients in September than in any other month of the year? He explained his answer. "There are so many people in Houston who work for fifty weeks at a miserable job, waiting for a two-week vacation. They go to Colorado Springs or New Orleans or Mexico City, spending all of their money, being miserable. They return to their homes with only one thought in mind: 'Now I have to go to work fifty more miserable weeks so I can go somewhere else to be miserable the other two weeks.' That's when I get my new patients." Then the psychiatrist said, "The problem is that a person who is basically unhappy in Houston will not really enjoy Colorado Springs. A person who is miserable most of the time in Houston will be miserable in New Orleans. And a fellow who is tired of living in Houston will get tired of Mexico City after a couple of days. The one thing that needs to be renewed is the one thing which we have neglected most—ourselves."

Is anything really new? Certainly, double-breasted suits are not new. Certainly, sideburns are not new. It is the person who grows the sideburns, admiring the image in the mirror. It is the fellow who buys the double-breasted suit, or the girl who wears the high-heeled shoes or the low-heeled shoes. The thing that ought to be new is the person—*you*. *You* are the thing that ought to be new.

Several years ago, I was invited to preach a revival at the Epworth Methodist Church in Houston. On the first evening, after the service was concluded, I was invited to join the congregation in the Fellowship Hall for punch and cookies. After a few minutes I made my way into the kitchen of the church. In the kitchen I saw a fellow that I had not met before. I walked over to him and said, "I'm Mouzon Biggs. I would enjoy meeting you." He told me his name. I could tell by the way he pronounced his name that he was not from my part of Texas originally. I asked, "Where were you born?"

He said, "I am from Argentina."

"That's great," I replied. "How long have you been in this country?"

"Well," he said, "I've wanted to be in this country since I was a small boy. From the time I learned how to read, I read stories about Texas. Finally, after I was married and had one son, I saved enough money to come to the United States. I said to my wife and son, 'I am going to Texas. I will work and make money and send for you.'"

I said, "Your wife and son must have been frightened to death. Texas is a long way from Argentina."

"Oh, no. They were not afraid," he said. "They know that I am a strong man."

"Well," I said, "how did you do in this new country?"

"I started trying to find work. I asked people for a job. I agreed to do almost any honest job for a fair day's pay. I was hired by this church. I saved my money as quickly as I could and sent it to my wife."

"She and the boy must have been very excited," I said.

"Oh," he replied, "I did not have enough for the boy. I sent only enough for my wife."

I said, "Your son must have been frightened to have his mother and father so far away."

"Oh, no," he said, "because I wrote to him and said, 'My son, we will make money; we will send for you. Stay with your grandfather.' My son knows that I am a strong man."

"Well," I said, "how did your wife like Texas?"

"Oh, she liked it fine. In fact, we were able to work harder as a team, and soon we sent money for my son."

"Well," I said, "that's great. Now the three of you were together again. How did your son like Texas?"

"Oh, fine," he said. "In fact, my son had been here only a week when all of the Boy Scouts from our church were going to summer camp. My boy wanted to go, too. The scoutmaster said no, because my son could speak no English. I explained that he would learn very fast. He would be a good scout."

"Did he enjoy scouting?" I said.

"Well, Mr. Biggs, in less than four years my son was an Eagle Scout."

"That's remarkable! That is truly remarkable! How did he do so well if he could speak no English?"

"Well, every night I would study with him. We would sit at the dining table. We would talk; he would study. He would get tired. Finally, he would say, 'Papa, can't we go to bed? I am so sleepy.' I would say, 'No, you study.'"

"Did he study?" I replied.

"Oh, yes, he studied, because he knows I am a strong man. He graduated number one in his class in high school. He received a five-year academic scholarship to Rice University."

During that four-day preaching mission, I came to know my new friend much better. The next winter, at Christmas time, my family received a beautiful card that said: "Christmas is a happy time. We are thinking of you. Your friend from Argentina." The following summer we received a lovely card that said: "We are taking a vacation, but we are remembering you, our friends." That card was mailed from Acapulco. Several weeks later I was preaching on television one Sunday morning when I told the story of our friendship. The following week he called me. He said, "I understand you preached about me on television."

"Yes," I replied, "but everything I said was very good."

"Oh, I know," he said. "I would like to buy your lunch."

He and I had lunch together. I finally said, "Are you no longer with the church?"

"Oh, yes," he said, "I am still with the church."

I said, "It is none of my business, but I do not know very many church custodians who can go to Acapulco on their vacation."

He said, "I now own a service station. I have been very careful about building a good credit rating. I saw the opportunity to buy a service station only a few blocks from the church. Now, when I sweep the front steps of the church, I look down the street to see if anyone is buying gas at my service station."

I said to him, "How have you done all of these things? You and your family have accomplished so very much in this new country. How?" He said again, "I am a very strong man."

"Well," I said, "what makes you so strong?"

He replied, "I am strong because I pray."

"You pray? When do you pray?"

"I pray many times, Mr. Biggs. I pray when I am sweeping the carpet. I pray when I am sitting up with my son trying to help him study. I know that he is tired, and I am tired, but he needs me. I pray because God has given me a new day and I want to be a new person in this day. I try never to miss a sunset, that I do not look and see. I try never to pass a child that I do not have a kind word. I do not pass a dirty man without hoping that he can be clean. I try to help my brother, and as I try, God makes me a strong man."

Is anything really new? Only one thing: A *person* can be new. Our Bible says, "If any man be in Christ, he is a new creature: old things are passed away" (II Cor. 5:17).

Our friend from Argentina will never make a million dollars at his service station, but he is already a very rich man. He is a rich man because he is a new person. He realizes that he is tied to all people, that he shares a common history with them. He knows that October can look like September, that April can look like May—unless a person is new and alive to each moment. Only then is something really new. *You* can know that newness in your own life!

What Do You Most Desire?

In a poll of the students of a certain college, one of the questions asked was: "What do you most desire?" A lot of them said they wanted to be popular. The word *popular* means to be held in high esteem, to be highly regarded. It means to be liked, or even loved; and truly, that is one of the deep desires of every normal person. In truth, success in life is largely determined by how well one is liked by other people. Many people fail not because of a lack of brains or ability, but usually because they do not get along with other people.

Every now and then, someone says: "Jesus was not popular." Do not believe it. He was the most popular man who ever lived. Everywhere he went people crowded around Him. Five thousand people followed Him into the wilderness on one occasion. People lined the streets when they knew He was coming. If He were the guest in a home, so many people would come they could not get inside the house. Even little children rushed to get into His arms. To be popular is a worthy ambition.

But popularity is like happiness. If you seek it, you never find it. The best way to get to sleep is to forget

27

about it—the same with popularity. The secret of being popular is losing yourself in something else.

Also, we must realize that there is no such thing as being liked by everybody. In the twelfth chapter of Romans, Paul says, "If it be possible . . . live peaceably with all men" (Rom. 12:18). Here he is implying that there are times when it is not possible to get along all the time. Not every person approved of Jesus, and some would even crucify Him. In fact, one is not completely popular with oneself. All of us have things that we ourselves do not like.

---◆---

Hope

It has been well said, "Life is full of glad surprises for those who hope."

One of the most famous paintings of all time is G. F. Watts' picture entitled *Hope*. It is the picture of a woman sitting on a globe. The idea is that this poor woman is fighting against the whole world. Her eyes are bandaged. She cannot see ahead. In her hands is a harp, but all the strings of the harp are broken save just one. Those broken strings represent her shattered expectations.

Now there is only one string left. It is the string of hope. Triumphantly she strikes that last string. From it there comes a glorious melody that floats out over her world and fills the dark night with stars. It is a great painting and a great truth. Even when all else is gone, if one will just continue to hope, things will work out.

Some years after he painted that picture, Mr. Watts received a letter from a woman to whom life had become unbearable. She was on the way to the river to drown herself. As she walked along the street, she saw some people standing before a shop window. She stopped and looked in. In the window was the picture *Hope*. She looked at the forlorn woman with her bandaged eyes and the broken strings. Then she saw the one string that was left, the string of hope. It so inspired her that she, too, struck the string within her own soul. She tried again and things went better. She concluded her letter to Mr. Watts by saying, "My children have long since discovered how much I love that picture, and they call it 'Mother's Hope.'"

When all the other strings of life are broken, we still have the string called hope, and when we strike it, things get better.

◆

Believe You Can

One of my minister friends tells of a man who nearly every Sunday would say to him, "Preacher, tell them they can—tell them they can." There is a story back of that man.

Despite the background of a fine family and a good start in life, he had made a miserable failure of himself. He felt that life was completely over for him, that he could do nothing, and he would just as soon die. But he met a man who took a great interest in him and who taught him the principle that if a man believes that he can, he can. This conviction completely changed his life.

There is nothing more important than believing that you can, and this is really one of the supreme messages of the Christian faith. Whoever you are, whatever failures there may be in your life, no matter how difficult and dark the future, you still can. Jesus looked into the face of a group of very ordinary men and told them that they could conquer the world. They believed Him and set about doing it. The Bible refers to those men as "these that have turned the world upside down" (Acts 17:6).

One of the finest sportswriters America has ever had was a man by the name of Hugh Fullerton. He tells a story about a manager of a baseball team. Many years ago he was manager of the San Antonio, Texas, baseball club. He had the finest team in the league, but they had lost seventeen of their first twenty games. It happened that there was a revival meeting going on near the ball park. This meeting was being conducted by a faith-healing evangelist who was attracting a lot of attention. Some people thought this man could perform any miracle, and the baseball team had heard about this preacher.

One night after the game, the manager told each member of the team to give him his two favorite bats.

They did, and he loaded the bats in a wheelbarrow and told the men to stay there until he got back. He was gone an hour or so. Finally he returned and jubilantly told the players that he had taken their bats to this faith-healing preacher, and the preacher had blessed each one of the bats. Now these bats had a strange power in them.

The next day, San Antonio played Dallas. San Antonio got thirty-seven hits and twenty runs, and from that day on, they were the team they could be, and they won the pennant.

Now what happened to those bats? The answer is nothing. Absolutely nothing. But something happened in the minds of those ball players. Each of those players had a new feeling that he could hit that baseball. Each went up to bat with an attitude of faith. When we get the idea that we can't succeed in life, we won't. But if we believe we can succeed, we will. We need to tell ourselves, *we can.*

◆

People—For Better or Worse

Graduation means setting goals for your life. One goal held by all of us is a genuine desire for happiness. Happiness seems to be elusive; yet all of us seek it.

The happiest moments you will ever know are those moments when things are going well between you and the persons around you. The most miserable moments you will ever know are those moments when things are not going well with you and those around you. If you are with someone whom you enjoy, then eating a hamburger together is great fun. If you are with someone when a conflict has arisen between you, even the best steak falls far short of satisfying. The way you deal with people has much to do with whether you are happy or not.

The Bible reminds us that we are God's people when we love one another. How can this love be expressed? How can we really deal with people? I propose three very simple guidelines.

First, treat each person as if he or she is important! Not only does everyone want to feel important, but God has created everyone to be important.

My parents have lived their lives in the oil fields of east Texas. I grew up six miles outside a town of less than six thousand people. Nonetheless, when I was in high school, I could walk around the town square on Saturday morning and have twenty people or more call me by name. They knew my family, where I lived, and what number I wore on the football team. I went to college in a city of 200,000 people. Then I went to college in a city of 650,000 people. After graduation from seminary, I moved to Houston, Texas. Houston is a wonderful place to live, but at one time there were 125,000 new faces in the greater Houston area every year. It is very easy to feel unimportant, a part of a multitude.

It is much easier to be in love with humanity than it

is to love one person at a time. And yet, all of us need to be loved as a person—one individual.

I remember when my wife and I first moved to Houston. One of the first things we located was a laundry. Methodist preachers need lots of laundered shirts. The laundry nearest us was advertising their services for twenty-seven cents per shirt. Three blocks away, another laundry promised to launder shirts for twenty-five cents each. We tried both of these laundries. Then the first dropped its price to nineteen cents per shirt. The second retaliated by dropping the price to fifteen cents. The war continued downward until one week my shirts were washed and ironed for nine cents per shirt. Needless to say, we were enjoying their competition. One Friday afternoon, I went by to pick up my shirts. A very bright girl called to me from behind the counter, "Good afternoon, Reverend Biggs. You like your shirts folded, with heavy starch. I will have them for you in just a moment." I went back to that laundry again, because I had found someone who was willing to deal with me as a person, an important person.

Everyone hungers for that kind of attention. If you are willing to give yourself in helping as many people as possible to feel important, your life will be the richer for it.

The next thing you need to do is to set a goal of relating genuinely to as many people as possible. Knowing a person's name is not enough. Our biggest problems arise with the people whose names we know very well. Most people are unhappy because of very bad relationships with those who should be closest to them. How long has it been since you have sat down with those you love the most, when no television or radio disturbed a good conversation? How long has it been since you talked with your parents without some kind of interruption? Maybe more important, how long has it been since you have really listened to them?

One night, I conducted a little experiment in my own family. I came home from work at the regular hour. We had dinner together, and then all of us went into the den. I pushed the button and turned off the television set. I said, "Tonight, no television and no radio. Tonight, we are going to be with one another. We can play games." We tried Old Maid for a while. That is a good card game for children only six and four years of age. Then we tried singing together. I am not a good singer, but we all tried. I was about to run out of ideas, when I said, "I know! Let's make cookies." My wife looked at me as if I had lost my mind. I said, "I remember that when I was a child it was fun to cook together." We went into the kitchen. Allison, my six-year-old, sifted the flour. Trey, my four-year-old, poured in the sugar. Gayle and I were the referees. Jason, only one year old, was pretty unconcerned about the whole thing. In a few minutes, we had hot cookies and milk. Jason was more interested now. Then we brushed our teeth, said our prayers, and tucked the children into bed. Gayle and I went back into the den and talked until after eleven o'clock. We had been married almost eleven years at the time. I did not know that we had that much to talk about. I can tell you only one thing—it was one of the finest evenings we had had in a long time. We were trying to be *present* to each other.

Being present involves caring—genuinely caring for somebody else. The New Testament talks about this kind of love as being a very unselfish love that involves putting oneself out on behalf of someone else, with no assurance that your efforts will ever be returned. If you are willing to try that, your life will be the richer for it.

All of us begin with high ideals. We may be willing to say, "All right! Every person is important." Second, "I will try to relate genuinely to as many people as I can." Then we get discouraged because we realize there are 2,000,000 people living within thirty miles of our homes. There are about 250,000,000 people in the United States. There are about 4,000,000,000 in the world. Soon we get the idea that our efforts are unimportant. That is the third important thing to remember. *You* can make a difference! One person's influence really does count.

Growing up near a small town has some advantages. It also has many disadvantages. One of the disadvantages is the fact that there is little to do for entertainment. Football is the biggest thing going in small, east Texas towns. When I reached the seventh grade, I decided to be a football player. I volunteered for duty weighing ninety-seven pounds. I practiced all year, but I never did get into a single game. The next year, I had gained fifteen pounds. Everyone else had gained twenty pounds. I practiced all year, but I did not get into one single game. My ninth-grade year, I got into two ball games, but we were more than thirty-five points ahead each time before the coach called for me. In the spring of my ninth-grade year, I joined the high school boys for spring training. The first day we had calisthenics, then grass drills, and then scrimmaging. The coaches picked twenty-two boys for the scrimmage. I was not one of the twenty-two. After a few minutes, I walked up behind the coach and said, "Coach, how about me?" He said, "You are too little." After a few more minutes, I asked him again. "Coach, how about me?" "You are too little," he replied. When the practice was over, I went into his office. I said, "Coach, I really do want to play football for Carthage High School." He told me some things to do. He had a recommendation for breakfast, for lunch, and for dinner. He recommended a careful program of lifting weights. Then I bought a pair of track shoes and began to run every afternoon. I continued that rigorous program for more than a year. It included a hard job for the three months of summer. In September of my junior year, I was working hard to make the team. The two linebackers playing ahead of me were twenty-five pounds heavier than I was. With only five days left before the first game, we had an injury in practice one afternoon. It was not serious, but one of the linebackers would be out for six weeks. The coach turned to me and said, "Mouzon, Friday night is your night." I will never forget it. We were playing a larger high school from Marshall, Texas. I remembered the first play from scrimmage. The coach had told me to hide behind the big defensive guard and defensive tackle playing in front of me. Our guard weighed 212 pounds, and our tackle weighed 215 pounds. I was supposed to watch the offensive guard to see which way the ball carrier was going. When the ball was snapped, their guard crossed out on our tackle. Their tackle crossed in on our guard. There was a huge, gaping hole and a 200-pound fullback coming straight toward me. I was scared. I was not afraid of being injured. I had worked almost five years for this moment. I *was* afraid that I might miss the ball carrier. The coach had reminded me many times that I could not depend on the halfback behind me. There was always the possibility that someone had blocked him to the ground. The coach had also reminded me, "Mouzon, you are not very big. When you see the ball, you charge." I charged!

Since that time, I have learned that our churches, schools, governments, businesses, and institutions are run by people no wiser and no stronger than you and I. They are run by people who may not be very big, but who are willing to charge!

All I am trying to say is this: *Do not underestimate what one person can do, with the help of God.* Go toward your goal of happiness with three important ideas about how to deal with people. *Believe in the importance of each person. Relate genuinely to as many as you can. Believe in the contribution one person can make, particularly when he or she allows God to work in his or her life.*

The Rhythm of All Life

A lovely lady tells of an experience that changed her entire life. She felt defeated, helpless, and afraid. She had gone off to a lonely spot on the beach to be away from everybody. She had thoughts of even ending her life. As she lay on the beach, she happened to put one hand on her wrist and she began to feel her own pulse. She noticed that her pulse had a definite rhythm. As she lay there feeling the rhythm of her own pulse, she looked out and saw the tall beach grass washed clean by the tide. A gentle breeze was blowing, and the grass was moving back and forth. To her astonishment, she realized that there was also a definite rhythm to the waving of the beach grass, and she further realized the rhythm was the same rhythm as the beating of her own pulse.

She raised her eyes a little and noticed the sea. She watched the waves as they came in, washing slowly over the white sands, spending themselves in bubbles on the shore. To her astonishment, she saw that there was also a rhythm in the waves of the ocean, and it was the same rhythm that she saw in the grass and felt in her own pulse.

Suddenly she saw a new truth. A human being, the

beach grass, and the mighty ocean are all a part of one great creation, with one God governing them all. If God could keep the sea and the beach grass healthy and normal, He could also do the same for her. Realizing that she was in time with the universe, she felt a new power. She felt that she was a part of the greatest thing in all the world. She found new strength and new reason for living.

Things Work Together for Good

Many bad things can happen to a person. But Paul once said, "All things work together for good to them that love God" (Rom. 8:28). He does not say that everything that will happen in your life will be good. But here is an illustration. The purpose of a ship is to go across the water; but there are parts of a ship that will not float—the engine, for example. Put it out on the water and it will sink. The propeller of the ship would sink if you put it on the water. Even the compass by which the ship is guided would sink if it were put on the water by itself. But when all the parts of the ship are built together, they will float.

So it is with life. Some things that happen are bad; some things hurt very deeply; but other things that happen to us are good. If we will take all of the experiences of life, both the good and the bad, and work them all together into one whole—like building a wall with many bricks—and if all our experiences in life are cemented together by our love for God, then the sum total of life will turn out to be good. We must not concentrate on just one sorrow or one disappointment or one tragedy. We must consider all of the experiences of life together as making up the whole of life.

There is a Greek legend that I think is wonderful. It is about a woman who came down to the River Styx to be ferried across to the Land of Departed Spirits. The kindly old ferryman was named Charon. He reminded her that it was her privilege to drink of the waters of Lethe, and thus completely forget the life she was leaving. Eagerly she said, "I will forget how I have suffered." But Charon reminded her, "You must also forget how you rejoiced."

She said, "I will forget my failures." He replied. "You will also forget your victories."

"I will forget how I have been hated," she said. "But also you will forget how you have been loved," he replied.

Then she paused to consider the matter, and the end of the story is that she would not drink of the water of forgetfulness. She preferred to retain the memory of sorrow and failure, and even hate, in order to keep the memory of joy and victory and love. As we look into the future, we would like to think of a life that would have no sorrows, tragedies, defeats, and hurts. But when we think of the other side, we are willing to take it all together. So as we face the future, we face it with anticipation instead of with fear.

Don't Be Afraid of the Gamble in Life

Look at one particular scene of Calvary. Christ is now hanging on the cross. The soldiers have stripped his garments and divided them among themselves. His seamless robe was left. It could not be divided, so they gambled for it (John 19:23, 24).

Looking at that scene, G. A. Studdert-Kennedy was inspired to write the following poem.

And sitting down, they watched Him there,
The Soldiers did;
There, while they played with dice,
He made His sacrifice,
And died upon the Cross to rid
God's world of sin.

He was a gambler, too, my Christ,
He took His life and threw
It for a world redeemed.
And ere His agony was done,
Before the westering sun went down.
Crowning that day with its crimson crown,
He knew that He had won.

There are three things I want to say about gambling: (1) *Life demands that every person gamble.* "He was a gambler, too, my Christ." And so am I, and so are you. Life is more—much more—than a game of chance; yet you cannot eliminate from life the gamble it demands. If you lived only in the past and in the present, you could live with certainty. You know what happened yesterday. You know what is happening at this present moment. But life not only has a past and present, but it also has a future, and that makes the gamble.

One of the disturbing facts of our generation is that we are exalting the word *security*. You find the word increasingly frequent in our everyday language. The term *social security* is well known to all of us. A civilization that devotes itself to taking the risk out of life will soon die, and should die.

Lin Yutang, the Chinese philosopher, looks at four centuries of our civilization. The seventeenth century brought forth the Reformation, as people sought the divine purposes of God. The eighteenth was a century of reason, and the nineteenth was a century of economic development. Now, he says, the watchword of the twentieth century is, "Give me security or give me death." Today we think of pensions, comfort, a job that will last, and of living to be old.

Columbus didn't put security first. Neither did the Pilgrims nor those who led the American Revolution nor those who packed their belongings in covered wagons and headed west. One day my schedule was such I could not go by car or train. I considered the risks in flying, but then I concluded, if I wouldn't take the risks, I couldn't make the journey. So it is with life.

I say to some couples at the altar of the church, "I now pronounce you husband and wife." What gamblers they are! Gambling their happiness on their faith in each other. By and by they decide to bring a baby into their home. That baby can grow up and break their hearts, but they take the risk. They save some money and make a down payment on a house. Something could happen so that they lose their investment, but again they take the risk. So it goes through life.

Now let's consider a second fact: (2) *The gamble of life is what brings excitement into our living.* Suppose someone came to me with a videotape that showed my entire future life from this moment until I die. I would refuse to look at it because it would rob me of all the thrills and the adventure.

Gambling is good, but like most other good things, it can be perverted and degrading. And that is what happens when we lose the high adventures of life. When life becomes dull and monotonous, many people turn to other forms of gambling—the racing of horses or dogs, the turn of a card, the roll of the dice, the outcome of a game—that sort of gambling is not so much sinful as it is silly. The gambler who perverts this God-given instinct to dream and dare in life and throws it away on betting dimes or dollars is a pitiful person.

Look at Calvary. Those soldiers at the foot of the cross that day rolled dice and got a momentary thrill. One of them even won a seamless robe. Some people never see anything higher than that. But then some look up and see Him on the cross—see One wagering a life because of His faith. As Studdert-Kennedy said, "He took His life and threw/It for a world redeemed."

Note this scene from the Bible: "Now as he [Jesus] walked by the sea of Galilee, he saw Simon and Andrew his brother casting a net into the sea: for they were fishers. And Jesus said unto them, Come ye after me, and I will make you to become fishers of men." Now notice carefully: "And straightway they forsook their nets, and followed him" (Mark 1:16-18).

Turn to another scene. "One came and said unto him. Good Master, what good thing shall I do, that I may have eternal life? . . . Jesus said unto him, . . . go and sell that thou hast . . . and come and follow me. But when the young man heard that saying, he went away sorrowful: for he had great possessions" (Matt. 19:16-22).

I do not know what happened to that rich young man. I suppose he was comfortable and secure the remainder of his life, but I imagine he also found life to be very dull and hardly worth living. We do know what became of Simon Peter. He gave up his boat, and he had some hard moments, but he had some thrilling experiences, too.

Wallace Hamilton has a sermon, "Wanted: Great Gamblers," from which I have taken several suggestions. In that sermon Dr. Hamilton quotes a little poem.

> Some men die by shrapnel
>   And some go down in flames.
> But most men perish, inch by inch,
>   Who play at little games.

The soldiers at the cross gambled for a robe. Their stakes were small, and they could not win much.

> He was a gambler, too, my Christ,
> He took His life and threw
> It for a world redeemed.

We can settle down with those soldiers and waste our lives on petty issues—a piece of clothing, representing the day-to-day living. On the other hand, one can look higher and see the Christ and be inspired to live for something eternally worthwhile. The more we are willing to risk, the more we stand to gain, and some people are willing to risk their lives.

Life demands that every person gamble, and the gamble of life is what brings excitement into our living. Now we must consider one more fact: (3) *The stakes you gamble for determine what you win in life.*

I have been to a horse race, but I did not bet on any of the horses. So, I neither won nor lost anything. But life is not like that. You can't just sit and watch it run by. You are compelled to wager on something. It is impossible to live staking your life on nothing. You may refuse to make up your mind, but you cannot help but make up your life. You may hold back your opinions, but you cannot hold back your character. We become something, whether we want to or not. And our characters and our lives are determined by the gambles we take with our lives.

The old English sailors used to sit on the rocky coasts and talk to the young men about the sea and the life of a sailor. They spoke not of the joy and pleasure. Instead, they talked of the dangers. They described the strong winds, the heavy storms, the high waves, and the dangerous rocks. They told of how a ship had to be strong to get back home and how sailors lost their lives in their dangerous adventures. Hearing the old sailors talk, those boys would run away from home, if necessary, to become a part of that life. It was the thrill of high adventure that they wanted.

So it was with our Lord. He never talked of the ease and comfort of the Christian life. He talked about self-denials and sacrifices. He said, "Whosoever will come after me, let him deny himself, and take up his cross, and follow me. For whosoever will save his life shall lose it; but whosoever shall lose his life for my sake and the gospel's, the same shall save it" (Mark 8:34, 35). "Do you dare to take the gamble with Me?" Christ is asking.

On what did He wager His life? He wagered His life on the fact that there is a God, that it is better to do right than to do wrong, that a life dedicated to God's will and purposes is not lost. The Bible says, "For the wages of sin is death; but the gift of God is eternal life" (Rom. 6:23). That is either true or not true. On which side do you wager your life? You can't be neutral. Suppose you bet against God and eternal life and suppose the Bible is true. Then what?

Christ wagered His life on the proposition that whatever we consecrate to God will not be lost. The rich young ruler took the opposite course and lived and worked for his own interests. One of the two made the wrong bet. With our lives we decide which one we believe was right.

> He took His life and threw
> It for a world redeemed.

The young ruler held on to all he had. We are kin to one or the other. Let's be sure to pick the one that is right, because our ability to pick the winner will be either our making or our ruin.

Donald Hankey said: "Religion is betting one's life there is a God." You can't just sit back and refuse to make up your mind. You must bet one way or the other. How do *you* bet?

The Timid Souls

In at least one city, there is a group that calls itself the Society for Timid Souls. You can get up quite a large membership for this society in any city. For many years a popular cartoon was the one about Caspar Milquetoast. He was a sad, unhappy, weak character personifying the inferiority complex.

One of the handicaps of life is extreme timidity. It is a handicap that is not easy to overcome. But there is a lot of help if one will only use it. One reason for our timidity is that we think about ourselves too much. Shy, timid persons relate everything to themselves. They keep themselves at the center of their thoughts. One thing we need is to get something bigger than ourselves to think about.

I know personally a young woman who overcame this extreme timidity. As a baby she was severely burned on the face. The burn left large and ugly scars, and as she grew older she became deeply conscious of those scars. She felt that everybody was laughing at her or pitying her. She had seven major operations on her face, which greatly improved her appearance, but she still had this extreme timidity. She was frequently disheartened and discouraged. But one day she read two statements that changed her entire thought process. Her old personality was not changed in just the reading of these two statements, but she kept them in her mind and gradually these two statements became the basis of a new personality for her. The first of these two statements is from the Bible. Paul said, "I can do all things through Christ which strengtheneth me" (Phil. 4:13). The other statement was from Ralph Waldo Emerson: "Neither you nor the world knows what you can do until you have tried."

◆

Blemishes Can Be Blessings

Booker T. Washington used to speak of the advantage of a disadvantage. He, himself, was an example. Born a slave, he used to carry the books of his white master's children to school. He wanted to go to school also, but the doors were closed to him. He developed such a passion for an education that he became one of the best-educated Americans of all time and founded a great university.

Often your handicap can be your blessing. Here is an illustration. Some time ago, a man wrote an article entitled "How to Work Your Way Out of Failure." He owned an apple orchard out in the mountains of the West. He used to advertise that apples grown in a cold climate and high altitude had firmer flesh and deeper flavor. He sold his apples to a very select clientele and would advertise them as perfect apples.

One year, just as his crop was ready to be harvested, a heavy hailstorm hit and left unsightly brown spots on the apples. The spots did not hurt the apples, but they looked imperfect. He could not afford to lose his apple crop that year, but a lesser man would have given up in defeat. He kept thinking and believing that there was a solution to his problem. Then one day an idea came to him. He picked the apples and put them in the boxes, as he had done every year. Then he put a card in the box, calling attention to the hail spots on the apples. He pointed out that these apples were grown in very high altitudes and sometimes sudden temperature changes bring hailstorms. He said that if you looked closely, you could even see the marks of the hail on the apples. It is a matter of record that the next year more than half his orders were for hail-marked apples. What first seemed to be blemishes turned out to be blessings!

Get the Picture

A certain psychology teacher would urge his students to sit quietly and conceive of their minds as a blank movie screen. Then he would say to them, "Flash on the screen of your mind the picture that you really want, then take it off. Flash it on again, then take it off. Flash it on again, then take it off. Do this over and over until that picture gets firmly fixed in your mind, then hold it there, and the picture will come to pass."

Being a Person Who Makes a Difference

Several years ago I was invited to address a convention of more than eighteen hundred persons at the Shamrock Hotel in Houston. As I took my place on the platform, I saw a huge banner at the back of the room, which said: THE CLUB FOR YOUNG MEN WHO WANT TO MAKE A DIFFERENCE!

All of us want to make a difference. All of us want to feel that our lives contribute something to the society in which we live. Are there certain qualities that guarantee that a person can make a difference? I believe there are. I want to mention four of these to you.

The first important quality is *enthusiasm*. People who are genuinely excited about what they are doing are people who make a difference.

There was a man in Houston named Walter Jenkins, a fascinating person. He was a song leader for the Billy Sunday revivals in Chicago in the early 1920s. Mr. Jenkins was Director of Music at the First Methodist Church in Houston for thirty-five years. Several years ago, he had a stroke. His health became a primary concern to all of those who loved him. Mr. Jenkins lost his son, Dick, a very capable Methodist minister, to a premature death from cancer. He also lost his wife, Vivian, who played a very important part in his life. Those three things are enough to make most men curl up and die. But Walter Jenkins was not like most men.

Mr. Jenkins came into the church one Monday morning, whistling as loudly as any man can whistle. Obviously, he was very happy. I said, "Mr. Jenkins, why are you whistling so loudly this Monday morning?"

He said, "I have been invited to lead the singing in a revival again."

I asked, "Mr. Jenkins, how old are you now?"

He smiled and said, "I am eighty-two, but that's all right. The preacher for this series is Dr. Clovis Chappell, and he is eighty-nine."

Several weeks after that, I came into the church one day after lunch. A couple was standing just inside the door. I asked, "Can I help you?"

They replied, "We're looking for Walter Jenkins."

I said, "Mr. Jenkins is retired now. He comes by the church to get his mail, but he is not here most of the time. I will be very happy to give you a telephone number."

They said, "We don't really need to see Mr. Jenkins. We just wanted to tell him that our church has never had a finer revival than the one we just had where our song leader was eighty-two and our preacher was eighty-nine."

The next Christmas, Mr. Jenkins was invited to conduct a musical worship service at the maximum security unit of the Texas Department of Corrections in Huntsville, Texas. When Mr. Jenkins walked onto the stage he was greeted with icy stares. However, within fifteen minutes, that group had been transformed by the personal magnetism of Walter Jenkins.

Walter Jenkins made a difference because he was excited about what he did. *You* be excited about what you do, and you will make a difference.

Even so, enthusiasm can run very shallow if it has nothing undergirding it.

The second quality that I ask you to have in your life is *courage*. *Courage* is a good word. It comes from the same root word as the French word for heart. A person who has courage is a person who has a little more heart than other folks seem to have.

I remember my first day as one of the ministers of the First Methodist Church in Houston. It was a Friday in June of 1967. On that first day, I was making hospital calls in several different hospitals. Late in the afternoon, I visited in the Methodist Hospital. I will never forget one of the patients I met that day. I knocked at the door of a woman patient. A gentleman came to the door. I introduced myself to him. He told me that he was the patient's husband and asked if I knew anything about his wife's illness. I said that I did not. He then told me that she was the victim of a severe stroke. She had been unconscious for more than two weeks. She was now conscious, but almost completely paralyzed. I asked if I might see her for just a few moments. He said, "Of course, she will be very glad to meet you. I just wanted you to know how very ill she is." When I walked to her bed, she tried to speak to me. Speaking was very difficult for her, but I finally understood one important question. She asked, "Mr. Biggs, what do I do now?" I am not a doctor. I do not pretend to be a doctor. However, several weeks before that day I had attended a seminar conducted by a doctor. He had told our group of ministers that a real stroke destroys a part of one's brain. The only way a person seems to recover from a stroke is to have good medical attention, probably lots of prayer, and the courage to teach the rest of the brain to pick up the function lost by the damaged portion. In this case, the damaged portion of the brain was that part that coordinated her muscles. The doctor had also told us that if feeling is ever to be restored, the feeling will first appear in the outer extremities—the fingers and toes. I did not go into all of that, of course. I simply said, "I do not know what you ought to do a year from now. But today you probably should try to wiggle the big toe on your right foot." She replied, "If you will pray for me, I will do that." Throughout the summer, our ministers called on her regularly. I remember seeing her one very hot day in August. The temperature in Houston was ninety-eight degrees, the humidity more than 90 percent. When I walked into the hospital, the cool air felt good to me, but when I entered her room the first thing I noticed was perspiration running down her temple. I said, "Do you feel all right?"

"Why, sure," she said. "Why not?"

"Well, you are perspiring."

She chuckled, and said, "Mouzon, I am more than sixty years old, and I have been downstairs lifting weights for almost an hour and a half."

One of the most thrilling moments in my ministry came on the Sunday evening before Thanksgiving in the fall of 1967. At the close of my sermon, I invited every person in the sanctuary to pray. I explained to the congregation how they could pray silently in the pews where they sat or they could come to the altar and join hundreds of others who would be praying silently there. Many came to the altar to pray, but one caught my attention. I saw her stand and then walk slowly to the altar—it was this same woman who knelt there to pray.

You do not have to feel sorry for this woman. She is a remarkable person. She has a little more heart than other folks seem to have. Courage is so very important.

Enthusiasm and courage are very important qualities, but both of these can run shallow without something deeper.

Let me explain a third quality by telling you an

experience I had when I was in seminary in Dallas. One of the outstanding persons who came to lecture at the seminary was Dr. Viktor Frankl. Dr. Frankl related many interesting experiences from his life. Prior to World War II, Dr. Frankl was a psychiatrist in Vienna, Austria. Because of his Jewish background, he was thrown into a Nazi concentration camp. Dr. Frankl described some of the horrors of those camps. The prisoners were forced to sleep on boards nailed to the sides of the walls. One man slept only six inches above another. In the summertime, they almost suffocated. In the winter, they almost froze to death. All year long the rats and cockroaches ran across their bodies while they tried to sleep. There was no medical care and very little food. Every morning before daylight, a guard banged on a bucket outside the building and shouted, "Get up, get up! It is time to work!" Dr. Frankl and the other prisoners knew that they were being kept alive only because they could work. They could help to rebuild bombed-out bridges, roads, and railways. Week after week, they saw hundreds of Jewish people being carried to their death. They knew about the ovens and the gas chambers. They knew about the mass graves where hundreds of bodies were dumped into open pits and covered by bulldozers. Some men grew sick after only three months; some more were gone after six months. Still others had fallen away by the end of nine months. At the end of the first year, only one man had been in Dr. Frankl's barracks as long as he had been there. Dr. Frankl decided to find out what kept this fellow going to work every day. His plan was to work alongside this man to see if he would talk to him about his inner strength. He soon discovered that his new friend enjoyed talking about his wife. He talked about the day they were introduced. He enjoyed recalling one of their first dates together. Then he described their wedding and the birth of their first child. He would always talk about how beautiful she was and how he could hardly wait to see her again. Then one day a new prisoner came into Dr. Frankl's barracks. He spoke to Dr. Frankl's new friend. The new prisoner told Dr. Frankl's friend that he had seen his wife taken to her death only days before. Dr. Frankl's friend grew quiet. He was no longer interested in anything. He would not discuss the horrible food, the hard beds, the cruel treatment, or his lovely wife. One morning, Dr. Frankl was awakened by the guard outside, beating on the can and shouting, "Get up, get up! It is time to work!" He reached down to shake his friend. The body was very cold. He had been dead for several hours. Dr. Frankl quickly performed a medical examination to see if this fellow had something that might kill the rest of the prisoners. He discovered that this man had had a dread disease for more than a year. As long as he had a tremendous desire to live, his body had stabilized that disease. When his desire to live was taken away, in less than sixty days he had died.

Dr. Frankl became a practicing psychiatrist again. He stated that a man can endure almost any *how* for living if he has a *why*. Dr. Frankl told the students at Southern Methodist University how so many people walk on the face of the earth without a *why* for their lives.

Why do you run? Where are you going? What do you hope to accomplish? What is the power, the meaning, the purpose of life? I would hope that you put your deepest trust in the one God and Father of us all.

This third ingredient, then, is what preachers call *faith*. It simply means: What do you trust with the largest questions of your life?

The fourth quality is *love*. I am glad that preachers are not the only ones talking about love today. Many outstanding songwriters are talking about love. Many plays and movies are talking about the real meaning of love. Everyone wants to be loved.

Several years ago on a Sunday evening, I was driving my family home after church. My son, Mouzon Biggs III, who was only three at the time, started whining and complaining about being tired. He wanted to get into his mother's lap. Gayle turned to the back seat, lifted him into her lap, and he snuggled into her arms. Then Allison began to complain. She was only five. She could not understand why her brother should have special treatment. Why couldn't *she* be in the front seat? I tried logic first of all. I explained to her that our car had bucket seats. Both buckets were full; there was no more room. She was not impressed. She kept on complaining. I suddenly remembered something that I had read not long before in a magazine. A writer commenting about parents and grandparents who have had the experience of buying presents for two children. Invariably one of the children will complain, "John's present is better than mine." The giver quickly responds, "Oh, no, it is not. Both gifts cost exactly the same—one is blue, one is green. That is the only difference." This writer pointed out that most children are not really impressed with the price of the gift. The real question being asked is simply this: "Grandmother, is there any chance you would love John more than you love me?" At that point, the giver is supposed to say, "Do you think I would ever love John more than I love you? I would not. You are my favorite twelve-year-old in the whole world. He is my favorite ten-year-old." Then you give him a special hug, and he is supposed to be happy with the whole situation. That's what I wanted to do for Allison. I whispered to her, "Allison, I have a secret. Come closer to me." When I felt her close behind me, I said, "It is not safe for me to hold you while I drive along the freeway, but I would like to do something special for you. When we get home, I would like to help you be the first one in bed." She said, "Daddy, would you?" I said, "Of course, I will. You'd better be ready. When I drive the car into the garage, I am going to turn around and grab you into my arms. We will run to the back door, unlock the door, get your pajamas on, brush your teeth, say your prayers, and tuck you into bed—first one in the family." Do you know what she did? She sat down in the back seat and sang "Old MacDonald Had a Farm" all the way home.

Now I have a secret for you. There was one person at our house that night who was happier than Allison. There is one thing greater than being loved, and that is the privilege of loving. Allison went to bed very happily, but her daddy was a little happier than she. I had had the privilege of taking into my arms one little red-haired girl and running as fast as I could to help her be the first one in bed. Most of all, I was trying to help her know that she is my favorite little girl in the whole world. I had the privilege of loving somebody.

How much of yourself are you willing to give on behalf of another person? Would you like to make a difference—a real difference? Be excited about what you do. Have a little more heart than anyone else seems to have. Base your enthusiasm and your courage on a genuine faith in One Almighty God and be willing to give yourself in genuine love for another.

In God's Hand

We must believe that nothing can happen that God cannot handle. I have on my desk a paperweight. It is a glass sphere filled with water. Sitting inside is a little man. There is a substance in the water that causes it to become very cloudy when it is shaken up. Sometimes when I get bothered or unhappy, I pick up this paperweight and begin to shake it. Then I begin talking to the little man. I say "Little Man, you are bothered. You are being shaken up. Your world is being shaken up. But, Little Man, I have you right here in my hand. I have your world in my hand, and I am able to hold it."

Then I hold it still for a few moments, and it all clears up inside. Then I say to my little man, "Little Man, you see you did not need to worry after all."

Of course, talking to my little man, I'm also talking to myself. I remember the words of the psalmist, "In his hand are the deep places of the earth" (Ps. 95:4). I think of the song, "He's Got the Whole World in His Hands." Realizing that my world and my life are in the hands of a loving heavenly Father gives me calmness and takes away my fears.

The One Way

Some years ago there was a movement of young people who were known as Jesus People. The Jesus People used a sign called "One Way." It is one finger pointing upward. They were symbolizing the words of Christ, "I am the way" (John 14:6). We are reminded of the words of the prophet Isaiah, who long ago told the people, "And thine ears shall hear a word behind thee, saying, This is the way, walk ye in it" (Isa. 30:21).

If we would walk the One Way, there are four things we must do.

1. *Be willing to surrender your will to His will.* The

question is always not what do I want, but what does God want of me.

2. *To know Christ's Way, we must know Him.* I've told many people to read the Gospel of Matthew. Read it slowly and deliberately ten times, and it will change your life. Many have told me of dramatic changes that did come over their lives through this experience. Just reading it one time is not enough. Your mind must be fully saturated. Familiarize yourself with Jesus, and you will know His Way.

3. *You must begin to walk.* There is a story about a young bear cub being puzzled about how to walk. This little bear said to its mother, "Shall I move my right paw first or my left or my two front paws together or the ones on the left side together and the ones on the right side together?" In reply, the mother bear simply said, "Leave off thinking and just start walking."

If you keep thinking about this problem and that problem and worrying about where you are going, pretty soon you will get so confused that you can't do anything. The thing to do is just to start walking the Jesus Way. As you take each step, God will reveal to you the next step. But if you get to worrying about whether or not you can walk in the Jesus Way, you will get all tangled up.

These three things enable you to do the fourth necessary thing, and that is *face the future with anticipation instead of apprehension.* Too many people squander their powers worrying about what is going to happen tomorrow. A physician made a study of the things his patients were afraid of. He discovered that 40 percent are afraid of things that never happen; 30 percent are fearful of past events they can now do nothing about; 12 percent have anxieties about their health and are afraid of some imaginary illness; 10 percent are afraid of what might happen to some loved one. He concluded that only 8 percent of the fears he found in his patients had real causes that needed attention. Ninety-two percent of all their fears were needless.

There is one thought pattern stronger than the fear pattern. So if we just begin walking the Jesus Way, by faith our fears will be left behind.